About The Author

Jean-Gabriel Paquette is an online instructor & business advisor teaching online business and marketing with video courses.

He's the founder of Paquette University, which is a platform with video courses to build a successful online business.

Paquette University is becoming the "go-to" platform of knowledge and education for online entrepreneurs.

More about our work:

Paquette University is developing and building a powerful, simple and easy platform that lets their users have access to knowledge and learn all the different aspects of entrepreneurship.

His students are able to decide what to learn and at which pace, on top of having straight forward content with no filler information, which makes the process enjoyable and simple.

© 2017 Jean-Gabriel Paquette. All rights reserved.

Disclaimers

No part of this eBook may be reproduced or transmitted in any form or by any means, electronic or mechanical, including photocopying, recording or by any information storage and retrieval system, without written permission from the author.

While we try to keep the information up-to-date and correct, there are no representations or warranties, express or implied, about the completeness, accuracy, reliability, suitability or availability with respect to the information, products, services, or related graphics contained in this eBook for any purpose.

Any use of this information is at your own risk. The methods describe within this eBook are the author's personal thoughts. They are not intended to be a definitive set of instructions for this project.

You may discover there are other methods and materials to accomplish the same end result. The information contained within this eBook is strictly for educational purposes. If you wish to apply ideas contained in this eBook, you are taking full responsibility for your actions.

The author has made every effort to ensure the accuracy of the information within this book was correct at time of publication.

The author does not assume and hereby disclaims any liability to any party for any loss, damage, or disruption caused by errors or omissions, whether such errors or omissions result from accident, negligence, or any other cause.

© 2017 Jean-Gabriel Paquette. All rights reserved.

Introduction

$100 or $1?

That's an obvious question, isn't it? Direct marketing does the same, but with products and services.

The only way to know how to capture your audience attention quickly and long enough for them to know all of your benefits is to learn how to do it.

What a chance, you will learn it in this e-book!

Entrepreneur Institute will show you exactly what needs to be done and how to do it with techniques that you can apply right now, that's what you really want, right?

Are you looking to boost your revenue? Do you need a fast and great way to reach your customers?

Direct marketing is all about directly reaching out to your customer with an offer they can't refuse, but how can you do that? This is what I will show you.

In this e-book, you will learn:

- Who's your target audience? What do they like and what are they looking for?
- What are your competitors currently doing to get their attention and sell them?
- How to build a strategy to present the perfect offer for your potential customer
- Why and when to follow-up after the initial contact
- Measure and adjust your offer / audience based on your ROI and results

Now that you're reading to learn, let's jump right away into the topic so you can get your business moving.

If you have any questions or concerns, please e-mail me at jeangabrielpaquette@gmail.com and I will make sure to answer you the sooner possible, all I want is your entire satisfaction.

© 2017 Jean-Gabriel Paquette. All rights reserved.

Marketing 101

The importance through time

Do you remember people arriving at your house five to six years ago with a handful of products?

Well, those people had a goal.

<u>Their goal was to sell off their products to potential customers.</u> We usually know this form of sale as door to door sales. However, we forget that this is one kind of marketing too. Direct marketing has been around for ages. This form of marketing is more personal compared to other forms of marketing.

This is because, in direct marketing, an organization is directly dealing with its customers. There are no intermediaries between the organization and its customers, thus, making it one of the most effective forms of marketing used by companies.

Success in direct marketing?

- Marketing tools can be considered as a form of nuclear power for an organization. If used properly and effectively, marketing tools can cause a stir in the world.
- Look at successful marketing campaigns by brands like Nike, Dove and so on. Why do you think these brands are so well known? <u>This is because they were successful in correctly using the different types of marketing tools available.</u>

The problem with marketing

The main problem with marketing today is incorrect usage of marketing tools. Marketers do not know how to use the marketing tools according to their advantage. Either they are stuck with traditional marketing tools or they just focus on modern marketing tools.

However, marketing can only be done right with the correct proportion and mix of marketing tools. <u>Marketers need to use both traditional and modern tools to embed the names of their brands into the heads of their customers.</u>

© 2017 Jean-Gabriel Paquette. All rights reserved.

There is no specific concoction for successful marketing. Successful marketing is possible through:

- Good market research.
- Knowing your customers, you should know what tool will effectively work for them.

Why direct marketing?

Why will you choose direct marketing? Why not indirect marketing? Well, the answer to this question actually depends on your product. It depends on the type of product you are selling to your customers. For example, banks make use of direct marketing the most.

They need clients to open up savings accounts. Hence, they have people who keep on making calls to potential customers. Some banks even opt for door to door sales.

Let us look at some examples of direct marketing which worked miraculously for some brands:

- **Land Rover invites:** Land Rover is already a renowned name in the automobile industry. But they had to do something out of the ordinary to make sure that people remembered them.
    I. Hence, during the opening of their Liverpool showroom, they sent invited in a box which contained a balloon. An invite was attached to the string of the balloon along with a marketing message.
    II. When a person opened the box, a balloon would float out of the box with a hanging invite. <u>Why would people not show up at the opening?</u>
- **Kitkat mail:** Nestle even pulled a direct marketing stunt for their chunky KitKat bars. The marketers behind nestle made it look like that a postman couldn't deliver a bar of KitKat because it is chunky and heavy.
    I. As a result, the postman left behind an apology letter. The recipients of this mail could exchange the mail for a bar of KitKat chunky.
    II. What would you have done if you ever received such a mail from Nestle?

© 2017 Jean-Gabriel Paquette. All rights reserved.

- **Schott Solar's warranty calendar**: Schott Solar is a company which produces solar panels with a warranty of 20 years. They needed to prove their point in the solar panel wholesale market. Thus, they started giving out a 20 year calendar.
    I. This calendar had to be attached to the wall and stuck out about 60 centimeters from the wall. Well, Schott Solar did really make their point clear.
- **Tylenol samples**: Marketers behind Tylenol usually send samples with their mails. After receiving a sample, a customer had chances of receiving coupons or discount vouchers. Moreover, the company has even created a pocket serving size of Tylenol.
    I. This size can be used by other companies to give to their customers. In this way, Tylenol is marketing their product using their own channel and they are using channels of other companies to develop their brand name.

Proof it works

These four examples are proof that direct marketing still works. Yes, many consider it as a traditional form of marketing. But people do not know that use of social media also falls under direct marketing. By using direct marketing, companies can measure the result of their efforts. On the other hand, if companies go for indirect marketing, they cannot exactly measure the benefit received from marketing activities.

For example, if a company opts to sign up for a billboard, they cannot measure the number of people affected because of the billboard. However, if a coupon is sent through the mail, and that specific customer returns to the store with that coupon; the company will be able to analyze the market more accurately.

Direct marketing, done in the right way

Now the question is how do you correctly conduct direct marketing?

Let us look at the different tools of direct marketing:

- **Direct Mail:** You probably already know this one. Direct mail is one of the most common tools of direct marketing.
    I. Direct mail usually includes catalogs, postcards and mails. Sometimes companies send leaflets to raise awareness among customers. Moreover, they even give out discount coupons to their potential customers to encourage them to try out new products.
    II. Companies may send direct mail to all potential customers in an area. In addition to that companies sometimes list down target customers in an area and send direct mail only to those specific people.

- **Telemarketing:** Telemarketing has been used by different companies for ages and it is still used by some companies religiously. Telemarketing involves listing down potential customers and contacting them over the telephone.
    I. Marketers try to convince customers to buy their products over the phone. This form of direct marketing can enable companies to grab a large volume of sales instantly. Moreover, telemarketing is an effective tool for calculating results of direct marketing.
    II. However, marketers have to dedicate their time and do some research for successful telemarketing. For telemarketing to work, marketers need to collect accurate customer data and match customer profile to product data.

- **E-mail marketing:** E-mail marketing is the easiest type of directing marketing. You do not have to invest a single penny for e-mail marketing except for the internet connection.
    I. The only input for e-mail marketing is time. E-mail marketing can be very effective because it can directly reach your target customers.

© 2017 Jean-Gabriel Paquette. All rights reserved.

II. E-mail marketing can be used to send promotional offers to generate new customers. It can also be used to keep existing customers informed.

- **SMS marketing:** SMS marketing has newly emerged as an efficient marketing tool. Telecommunication companies offer a bundle offer to companies at a very cheap rate.
  I. Moreover, there are other companies who specialize only in SMS marketing. These companies already have a database which companies can use to send promotional text messages.
  II. Companies can even make their own databases by collecting phone numbers from their customers. Through text messages, companies can inform their customers instantly about new offers or products.

- **Direct selling:** Direct selling is the perfect marketing tool for low-cost flexible businesses.
  I. An independent salesperson visits a customer's house or workplace and sells products by hand.
  II. In face to face interactions, marketers have a very high probability of securing a sale.

- **Social media marketing:** Social media marketing is on the rise these days. This type of marketing is one of the most efficient and cheapest. Social media has opened a lot of doors for businesses to showcase their products.
  I. Moreover, customers can share products and expand the reach of products exponentially. Furthermore, thousands of people can easily be reached without creating a database.
  II. Thus, it is one of the most effective forms of marketing.

List down your prospects

The success of your marketing campaign highly depends on the creation of a reliable customer database. You cannot send postal mails or emails to random people.

You need to know whether these people actually have a chance or becoming your future customers.

Firstly, you will need to fix a customer profile. If you are a cosmetics brand, you need list down women who are interested in beauty. If you are selling luxury cars, you will need to list down women who have a high paid job or have a high expense household.

Who's your target market?

You will need to identify the interests of your target group and create a customer profile. Your customer database will consist of people with a similar customer profile.

You will also need additional information for your customer database. Your database should reflect the demographics of your target group.

You should also tap into information like:

- Which items did they purchase recently
- How much do they spend in each transaction
- How long do they wait before making another purchase

By looking at all the above, you will be able to read your customers. Moreover, <u>it will also give you an edge</u>. If you know that your prospect purchases frequently, a little persuasion from your end might lead to a sale.

Enhance your customer value services to turn your prospects into customers and to retain them in the future. Personalized messages and value added products will take you a long way.

© 2017 Jean-Gabriel Paquette. All rights reserved.

Get to know your target market

It is impossible for any brand to target everyone.

You know everyone will not buy your product. However, a specific group of people has high chances of choosing your product over a similar product.

For example, a Mercedes is not everyone.

This brand knows that only people with a high income can afford their products. Hence, they keep on targeting a high-income group. Thus, all their marketing is directed towards luxury. Similarly, you also need to find your target market.

How will you define your target market in a world where there are about 7 billion people?

Identify your target market

- **Look at your current customers:** <u>Firstly, you will need to look at your current customer base.</u>
    I. Who is buying from you?
    II. Why are they buying your product?
    III. Why are they choosing your product over other products? Identify common interests and traits within these people.
    IV. Which interest of theirs makes them use your product? It is highly possible that this very interest could also entice other people to use your product.
- **Know your product:** Firstly, you will need to know what makes your product unique. **You can start by noting down all the features of your product.**
    I. Then identify the benefit the customer can receive from each particular feature.
    II. Think of it in this way, you are a graphics designer and you offer higher quality designs to your customers. The feature that you are providing to your customers is high-quality designing services.

© 2017 Jean-Gabriel Paquette. All rights reserved.

III. Now, what benefit will they receive from your service? They will gain the attention of more people by using your unique, original and high-quality designs which in turn will help them make more money.
IV. Once you know the benefits your customers can receive from your products, make a list of people who need those benefits.

- **Select demographics for your target market.** By looking at your customer base and analyzing your product, you will understand who needs your product. But you will have to select certain demographics too. How do you select demographics? You look at people who have the highest probability of buying your product.
    I. **Age**: Which group of people is most likely going to buy a product? Hello Kitty is a character loved by all girls but not women. Thus, the marketers behind Hello Kitty know that their target group exists between ages of 6 to 17.
    II. **Location**: Location is also a very important demographic. If you are the producer of fur coats, you know that your products will have a higher demand in colder regions rather than warmer regions.
    III. **Gender**: Some products are very gender specific. If you are selling razors for men, you cannot include women in your target market.
    IV. **Income**: You can refer to the Mercedes example to understand the importance of this demographic.
    V. **Ethnicity**: You need to know exactly who uses your products. Is it African Americans? Is it South Asian people? Or is it people from England?

- **Take psychographics in consideration**: What is psychographics? Well, psychographics denotes the personal interests and traits of your customers. Psychographics include
    I. **Behavior**
    II. **Lifestyle**
    III. **Interests**
    IV. **Personality**
    V. **Attitude**

Psychographics will help you determine how your product or service fits into the lifestyle of your customer. It will also help explain when he or she uses it. You will be able to make your marketing techniques more effective.

© 2017 Jean-Gabriel Paquette. All rights reserved.

This is because by looking at psychographics; you will know from which media your customer collects information about your product. In this way, you will get to communicate with your customers through their chosen media.

- **Evaluate your target group**: With all the aforementioned tips, you will be able to recognize your target group. You need to be sure of your target group. Thus, you need to answer some questions to evaluate your decision:
    I. Do you have sufficient people who meet the criteria?
    II. Can your target group afford your product or service?
    III. Do you know what makes your target group reach for your product or service?
    IV. Is your product or service beneficial for your target group?
    V. Is your target group easily accessible?

Analyze your target market closely and if you do not reach to positive answers for all the questions mentioned above; rethink your target group again. A specified target group will lead to better marketing results. You do not want to waste your precious dollars on inefficient marketing.

© 2017 Jean-Gabriel Paquette. All rights reserved.

Keep a close eye on your competitors

Keep your friends close and your enemies closer.

This applies to every active business in the industry. Nowadays, there is so much competition in the market that if you close your eyes for a minute, you will miss something important.

Remember, you do not want to ignore your competitors.

If Mark Zuckerberg had overlooked the creators of MySpace, Facebook would not be what it is today. You should know every move of your competitor.

Competition is actually good for your business. Do you know why?

Well, firstly, it will help you see things from a new angle. Moreover, you will be able to recognize your own flaws. When you recognize your flaws, you will be able to work on them and make your business more successful. To analyze your competitors you need to:

- Who are your competitors? You need to identify your competitors. If you own a restaurant specializing in pizza, your competitors are all other pizza places.
    I. **However**, if you are the owner of an online cosmetics store, a store which sells cosmetics but has no online presence is not your competitor.
    II. **Thus**, identify your competitors carefully. Remember, your competitors and you share the same target group.
- **Identify their unique selling proposition.** You need to know what benefit your competitors are offering to your target group.
- **Find out how they operate in the market.** You can get ahead of your competitor by knowing how they operate in the market. You would want to collect information on their marketing techniques.

© 2017 Jean-Gabriel Paquette. All rights reserved.

I. **For example**, you own a clothing store. Your competitor only sends e-mails and postal mails for marketing. You can take advantage of this. You can market your clothing products on the social media and gain more exposure.
- **Analyze their campaign structure**. If your competitors' campaigns are peppy, then your competitors are very confident. However, if their campaigns are orthodox, it means that they are scared of trying new things.
  I. **Moreover**, frequent change in campaign structure suggests campaign failure. You can re-evaluate and re-organize your own marketing campaigns by looking at your competitors.

Build a marketing strategy

No structure, no results

You definitely need a proper marketing strategy if you are adamant on creating a successful marketing campaign. Without a properly organized structure, chances are that your campaign is not going to be very efficient.

But you want to make every dollar count right?

For an effective marketing strategy, you need to:

- **Identify your company's unique selling proposition.**
    I. Every company has a unique selling proposition. You need a unique selling proposition to develop a marketing strategy.
    II. Your unique selling proposition will make you stand out from the crowd. Take the Olympics games as an example. Nothing can be compared to this game. This is because both the athletes and the audience gain an unforgettable experience.
- **Identify your target market. You need to filter out your target market. You already know how to do this.**
    I. Just follow the steps and carve out your target market
- **Focus on your products.**
    I. By now you should already know the benefits that your product or service can give to the customers.
- **Create a marketing plan for positioning your brand in the market.**
    I. Without a detailed marketing plan, you will be swimming without a life jacket in the ocean.
- **You need to select certain marketing methods.**
    I. You can choose indirect marketing or direct marketing or even public relations.

© 2017 Jean-Gabriel Paquette. All rights reserved.

Imagine that you are going on a road trip. You have to plan ahead before going on a road trip. That is your marketing strategy. <u>The map for the road trip is your marketing plan and the resources needed to travel are your marketing methods.</u>

You need a thorough marketing plan because it will assist your marketing strategy. Moreover, you need relevant marketing methods to assist your whole marketing plan.

Finally, for a full proof marketing strategy, you also need to decide on a measuring technique.

If you are going to market your product, you need to measure the results of your efforts.

This is because if you are getting the results you desire, you might need to change your marketing strategy. <u>At the end of the day, it is your business and you need to maximize your profits.</u>

© 2017 Jean-Gabriel Paquette. All rights reserved.

Tempt your customers with an offer

A lot of big names in the market are falling down.

Survival in this tough competition is very difficult. Thus, if a new entrant wants to enter the market, the company needs to draw the attention of its customers instantly.

If you are the owner of a new business, you need to catch the attention of your customers right away. You need to tempt them with an offer which they cannot say no to.

Your customer will not be able to look away when he or she sees an unbelievable special offer. Yes, a special offer can give an instant boost to your sales. In fact, you can let know your consumers about this special offer via direct marketing methods.

Think of it in this way, you want a makeup product really bad.

However, you have to pay a hefty price for the product. But once you see there is a special discount of 20 percent on the product, you will not be able to resist yourself.

If you just put up a special offer without any marketing, it will not work. If you do not spread a word about your offer, how will people get to know about it?

You can promote your offer in the following ways:

- **You can spread word through postal mail or email.** Email is a direct marketing method.
    I. You just need to gather up the e-mail addresses of your target market and send them an e-card with your offer on it. There is technically no cost for this type of marketing

- **Use social media to publicize your offer.** You can create hype for your product or service by using social media.
    I. By spending some bucks on social media, you can get massive exposure. You can use Twitter, Facebook and Pinterest to promote your offer.

© 2017 Jean-Gabriel Paquette. All rights reserved.

- **Team up with other businesses.** You can collaborate with another brand for an offer. For example, you have an ice-cream parlor.
    I. You can collaborate with a restaurant nearby your parlor and give away a 20 percent discount coupon to customers dining in that restaurant. The customers are definitely going to pay you a visit because after a delicious dinner, they will crave for some ice-cream and they will also be saving some money!

- **Keep repeating.** Sometimes you need to keep on bombarding the customer with the same information. Repetition sells!
    I. You need to keep on letting your customers know about your offer again and again through direct marketing tools.

- **Knock on the doors of your existing customers!** Your existing customers are your most promising customers.
    II. Thus, when you have a special offer in hand, knock them first and then move onto new leads. Your existing customers already know of your brand and thus they are most likely to react to your offer immediately.

© 2017 Jean-Gabriel Paquette. All rights reserved.

Do not forget to follow up

The biggest mistake marketers make is that they forget to follow up.

Marketers only stress about creating a marketing strategy and informing the public about their product or service. However, they forget a very crucial step which is following up.

This is important because follow ups can generate future sales.

It is a knock on the door to remind your customer about your product or service. A study has shown that marketers do not follow up on about 40 to 50 percent of sales leads.

Failing to follow up on a sales lead is a loss for the company. You might have just missed a sale because that one customer could be really interested in your brand. Here are some tips which you can follow

- **Invest in follow-up techniques.** You do not have to follow up yourself. Hire some someone to follow up on customers. Follow-up may not be fun. But who told you that you need to do it yourself?
    I. You can invest in an auto-responder software. There is software in the market which can help you follow up with all your customers. You can schedule follow-ups on these software. Moreover, you can set reminders too. Investing in such a software can save a ton of time for you
- **Do not wait to follow up.** You need to follow up on new leads immediately. You cannot expect your customer to remember you after a couple of weeks. This is because he or she may be really busy.
    II. Thus, it is best not to wait for a follow-up. Follow-up immediately so that your customer still has a fresh memory about your product or service. Following up after a day or two or even a week can really impress your customer.

© 2017 Jean-Gabriel Paquette. All rights reserved.

- **Maintain relationships with your customers even after a sale.** You can use your auto responders to maintain relationships with your loyal customers.
    III. You can keep on adding value to your product or service by keeping an after sale relationship.
- **Keep a follow-up strategy in advance.** To save your precious save, create follow up sequences in advance. You might not always have the time to follow up. Thus, you can arrange your follow-up materials beforehand.
    IV. If you have an event coming up, you can create a follow-up e-mail structure and thank you note cards beforehand. After the event, you can add some details from the event to the e-mails and send them! Remember, time is money.

© 2017 Jean-Gabriel Paquette. All rights reserved.

Measure your success

Let us face the harsh truth.

Direct marketing will cost you some bucks. Your work does not end right after sending a few postal mails or the e-mails. It does not end even after replying to your customers' queries. You need to use every dollar efficiently. You need to know whether your campaign is bringing in good enough sales.

There is no point of just gaining likes and comments on your social media posts.

You need to know your return on investment. Why would you invest more if this method is not working for you? For every directing marketing tool used, you can measure your success rate.

The best mechanism for measuring your return is the response mechanism. If you send out postal mails or e-mails, you can count the responses you received from your potential customers.

For example, you sent out a mail with a reply form. The number of reply forms received is the total number of responses you received. Similarly, if you had provided a phone number, you could tally the number of phone calls received on that specific number after your direct marketing campaign.

You can ask these questions to calculate responses:

- How many responses did you receive within the direct marketing campaign period? You can count this from your mails, e-mails, responses from Facebook or Twitter and so on
- How many of those responses actually turned into actual leads? This means how many of your target customers wanted to know more information about your products.
- How many of your leads turned into actual sales?

Now there are three ways in which you can calculate your return on investment:

- **Cost per acquisition**: The cost per acquisition can be calculated very easily.

© 2017 Jean-Gabriel Paquette. All rights reserved.

I. Firstly, you will need to calculate the total cost of your direct marketing campaign.
  II. Secondly, you will need to calculate the total responses received from your campaign.
  III. If your total cost is around USD 1000, and you received 10 responses, this means that your cost per acquisition is USD 100. This indicates that the cost behind every customer is USD 100. You can use this measure to identify whether the cost behind every customer is in line with your profits.

- **Cost per piece**: The cost per piece is an indicator of the cost involved in reaching every single potential customer.
    I. You can find this out by calculating the total cost of the campaign.
    II. Then you will have to divide the total number of mails sent by the total cost.
    III. If the total cost is USD 1000, and the total number of mails sent is 100, your cost per piece is USD 10. By lowering the cost per piece, you will be able to mitigate your cost per acquisition.
- **Response rate**: The response rate is an important indicator of direct marketing too. By calculating the response rate, you will be able to identify the actual success rate of your campaigns.
    I. Think of it in this way, if you had sent out 1000 mails and only 10 people responded, the response rate of your marketing campaign will be 1%.
    II. If you are not happy with a response rate of 1%, then you need to go for an aggressive campaign. You might want to re-arrange your potential customer mailing list.

By calculating your return on investment, you will be able to know what to do next.

If you are happy with your return on investment, you can continue using the same technique. However, if you are not satisfied, then you can change your techniques.

You can change your tagline, marketing tool or mailing list to get better results.

The best way to reach your audience

Direct marketing or precision marketing is more effective than mass marketing.

You are already aware of the advantages it offers compared to other forms of marketing. In other forms of marketing, it is quite difficult to analyze and interpret results but not in direct marketing. Direct marketing allows you to grow stronger bonds with your customer. It also allows you to retain your customers.

What is the point of marketing if you do not get to know whether it is working or not?

How can you own a successful business without knowing whether you are expenditure is worth it or not? This is where direct marketing comes in. You can prepare a cost-benefit analysis with the help of direct marketing and act accordingly.

Remember, you need to test the water before getting into it.

There are two sides of every story. Direct marketing does have a few cons:

- If you had chosen e-mailing as your marketing tool, chances are that your emails might end up in the junk folder.
    I. In addition to that your emails might even be considered as spam. In telemarketing, sometimes the phone calls can get a bit awkward and cold.
- Sometimes telemarketers try to force their customers to buy products and this type of behavior is not welcomed by the customers.
- Social media marketing can give you a lot of exposure but everyone does not use a smartphone. Moreover, a lot of people do not trust the internet.

Everything has a bad side and a good side. But when it comes to direct marketing, the pros weigh more than the cons. **If you are an entrepreneur who is looking to market his first product then direct marketing is your key.**

Even if you are the owner of a big business, you need direct marketing to retain your customers. You need to constantly keep in touch with your customers to remind them that you are there.

What better way to do it other than direct marketing?

© 2017 Jean-Gabriel Paquette. All rights reserved.

Conclusion

I want to thank you for reading this e-book and learning with us, I hope it was a great experience for you!

If you have any questions or concerns regarding what you just learned, please send me an e-mail to jeangabrielpaquette@gmail.com , I will answer you the sooner possible. I aim for customer satisfaction.

Mark my word, I will help you until you're satisfied with the service I provided! I want you to be happy and grateful of this new knowledge.

I will always deliver on point, good and useful content to my customers!

Was this e-book beneficial to you?

If it was, please leave an honest review. That's all I ask from you!

Now that you learned about how to create an effective direct marketing strategy. Apply your new knowledge right way and make good use of your new knowledge.

© 2017 Jean-Gabriel Paquette. All rights reserved.

www.ingramcontent.com/pod-product-compliance
Lightning Source LLC
Chambersburg PA
CBHW070720210526
45170CB00021B/1392